KINGDOM BUSINESS

52 Biblical Principles for GODLY Leadership & Wise Decisions

Gerard Assey

KINGDOM BUSINESS:
52 Biblical Principles for
GODLY Leadership & Wise Decisions
By
Gerard Assey

Published by:
Gerard Assey
19/18, Palli Arasan Street
Anna Nagar East
Chennai - 600 102

ISBN: 978-81-989262-3-4

Table of Contents

Introduction
Welcome to Kingdom Business!

If you're a business owner, entrepreneur, CEO, manager, or leader navigating the pressures of decision-making, responsibility, people, performance, and purpose—this book is for you. But this isn't just another business book. This is a spiritual blueprint—a compass to help you build and lead not just profitably, but powerfully under God's direction.

In today's world, leadership often leans heavily on logic, trends, and ambition. But Kingdom leadership is different. It flows from divine wisdom, thrives on God-centered values, and leaves behind a legacy that extends far beyond profit margins. Kingdom business is not about sprinkling faith over commerce—it's about bringing Christ to the center of every business decision, every strategic plan, every conversation, every risk.

This book was birthed from the deep conviction that God's Word contains everything a leader needs to succeed righteously and lead courageously—even in today's cutthroat, fast-paced marketplace.

Purpose & Objective of This Book

This book exists to equip you to:

- ✓ Lead your business with clarity and conviction, rooted in biblical truth.
- ✓ Make God-honoring decisions that reflect the character and priorities of Christ.
- ✓ Build a legacy of integrity, impact, and influence that glorifies God and inspires others.

- ✓ Develop a weekly rhythm of reflection, prayer, and Spirit-led action in your leadership.
- ✓ Understand that your company or position is not just a job—it's a calling and Kingdom assignment.

Whether you're in a boardroom, on a factory floor, in a home office, or managing a global enterprise—you are called to be a steward, not just a strategist. This book will guide you through what that means practically and powerfully.

How to Use This Book

This book is designed as a 52-week journey—one biblical business principle for every week of the year. Each weekly entry contains:

- ✓ A Scripture-Based Principle – A key verse from the Bible addressing a real-world leadership or business theme.
- ✓ Reflection – Five deep-dive insights to meditate on. These are not just commentary but prompts to renew your mind and reset your business worldview.
- ✓ Application – Simple, practical steps to put the principle into action in your business or leadership context. These turn inspiration into transformation.

You can read the book:

- ✓ Week by week as a devotional, reflection, or planning tool.
- ✓ With your leadership team as a source for faith-based discussions.
- ✓ Individually or in small groups as a discipleship guide for business leaders.
- ✓ In focused study blocks—such as monthly retreats or strategic planning days.

Tip: Keep a journal or note section where you track how each week's principle shows up in your real-life leadership decisions.

Key Benefits for You as a Leader

By committing to this yearlong journey, you will:

- ✓ Develop a Kingdom mindset that will set you apart in an often self-centered business world.
- ✓ Gain confidence in decision-making, knowing your choices are anchored in God's Word.
- ✓ Build a culture of godliness and excellence within your organization.
- ✓ Learn to discern God's will amid market chaos, pressure, or personal doubt.
- ✓ Grow as a servant leader who reflects the nature of Christ—compassionate, courageous, and committed to truth.
- ✓ Leave behind a legacy not just of success, but of significance that echoes into eternity.

Final Encouragement

The marketplace is one of the greatest mission fields of our time. God is raising up Daniels in boardrooms, Nehemiahs in project management, Josephs in finance, and Esthers in executive leadership. If you're reading this, you are likely one of them.

This is not just a book—it's a commissioning.

Welcome to Kingdom Business.

Let the journey begin—with the Word of God as your strategy manual, the Holy Spirit as your guide, and Jesus Christ as your CEO.

WEEK 1:
Integrity is Non-Negotiable

Scripture:
"The integrity of the upright guides them, but the unfaithful are destroyed by their duplicity." –
Proverbs 11:3 (NIV)

Reflection:
- ✓ Integrity is not optional; it is foundational for long-term success.
- ✓ Leaders of integrity build trust—internally with teams and externally with clients.
- ✓ Shortcuts may offer temporary gains but lead to lasting damage.
- ✓ God honors businesses that walk uprightly, even when it costs.
- ✓ Integrity simplifies decision-making by removing compromise.

Application:
- ✓ Evaluate existing processes: Are there any ethical gray areas?
- ✓ Make transparency part of your company culture.
- ✓ If an opportunity requires compromise, turn it down—God will honor it.
- ✓ Address internal corruption promptly.
- ✓ Lead by example: Never promise what you can't or won't deliver.

WEEK 2:
Plan, but Submit Your Plans to God

Scripture:
"Commit to the Lord whatever you do, and He will establish your plans." – **Proverbs 16:3 (NIV)**

Reflection:

- ✓ Planning is godly, but our plans must be committed to God.
- ✓ Divine alignment brings lasting success—not just human intelligence.
- ✓ God may redirect your path for greater impact.
- ✓ Business strategy is best developed in prayer and partnership with God.
- ✓ Trust in God's establishment, not just in your execution.

Application:

- ✓ Begin every quarter with prayer-led strategic meetings.
- ✓ Involve godly mentors in reviewing business plans.
- ✓ Use this principle in project launches, expansions, and major investments.
- ✓ Train team leaders to develop "prayerful planning" habits.
- ✓ Keep a journal to track how God redirects or affirms your plans.

WEEK 3:
People Before Profit

Scripture:
"Carry each other's burdens, and in this way you will fulfill the law of Christ." – **Galatians 6:2 (NIV)**

Reflection:

- ✓ People are not tools—they are treasures.
- ✓ Businesses that value people will always attract loyalty.
- ✓ Serving others is a spiritual principle that brings unseen dividends.
- ✓ Prioritizing people builds a culture of care, which increases performance.
- ✓ Jesus put people before convenience—leaders must do the same.

Application:

- ✓ Create employee assistance programs or crisis support systems.
- ✓ Build customer care practices that go beyond basic service.
- ✓ Review HR policies: Are they compassionate or just functional?
- ✓ Visit your frontline workers and listen to their needs.
- ✓ Show up personally for team members in times of loss or need.

WEEK 4:
Build with Wise Counsel

Scripture:
"Plans fail for lack of counsel, but with many advisers they succeed." – **Proverbs 15:22 (NIV)**

Reflection:

- ✓ Isolation is dangerous for decision-makers.
- ✓ God uses people to give wisdom—seek it actively.
- ✓ Pride resists counsel; humility embraces it.
- ✓ Not all counsel is godly—discern between godly advice and worldly suggestions.
- ✓ Collective wisdom leads to stronger, sustainable strategies.

Application:

- ✓ Set up a personal board of spiritual and business mentors.
- ✓ Make collaborative decision-making part of your company's DNA.
- ✓ Encourage brainstorming and open feedback from all levels.
- ✓ Review major plans with at least 2–3 godly advisors.
- ✓ Use counsel especially in HR decisions, mergers, legal matters, or crisis situations.

WEEK 5:
Be Diligent, Not Lazy

Scripture:
"The plans of the diligent lead to profit as surely as haste leads to poverty." – **Proverbs 21:5 (NIV)**

Reflection:

- ✓ Diligence attracts divine blessing—sloppiness doesn't.
- ✓ God rewards persistence and hard work—not just passion.
- ✓ Hasty decisions often lead to avoidable losses.
- ✓ Diligence involves daily discipline, not just occasional hustle.
- ✓ A leader's diligence sets the pace for the entire organization.

Application:

- ✓ Establish systems of accountability and performance.
- ✓ Reward consistency and diligence—not just flashy results.
- ✓ Avoid rushing big decisions just to meet deadlines.
- ✓ Schedule focused work time—free from distractions.
- ✓ Teach your teams to do "heartily as unto the Lord" in all tasks (Col. 3:23)

WEEK 6:
Stewardship, Not Ownership

Scripture:
"The earth is the Lord's, and everything in it, the world, and all who live in it." – **Psalm 24:1 (NIV)**

Reflection:

- ✓ You are a steward, not the owner – Everything you have (your company, money, influence) ultimately belongs to God. You are entrusted to manage it well.
- ✓ True stewardship leads to accountability – A faithful steward seeks to multiply what's been entrusted while remaining answerable to the Master.
- ✓ Ownership mentality leads to pride and control, while stewardship cultivates humility and partnership with God.
- ✓ Stewardship impacts how we treat resources, people, and opportunities—with care, excellence, and foresight.
- ✓ God's approval is more important than shareholder praise—aim to hear "Well done, good and faithful servant."

Application:

- ✓ Begin financial reviews by acknowledging God as the true owner of the business.
- ✓ Reevaluate how you're using time, money, and personnel—are they being maximized for Kingdom purposes?
- ✓ Delegate responsibility with trust, knowing you're managing what belongs to God.

- ✓ Reflect before every major investment: "Is this good stewardship or personal ambition?"
- ✓ Reinforce this principle across leadership levels—change “my department” to “my stewardship.”

WEEK 7:
Excellence Reflects the Kingdom

Scripture:
"Whatever you do, work at it with all your heart, as working for the Lord, not for human masters." – **Colossians 3:23 (NIV)**

Reflection:

- ✓ Excellence is a form of worship—when done unto the Lord, even routine work becomes sacred.
- ✓ A spirit of excellence sets Christian businesses apart—it's not perfection, but wholehearted pursuit of quality.
- ✓ Excellence builds trust, enhances reputation, and reflects the nature of our perfect God.
- ✓ Sloppiness and mediocrity dishonor both the brand and the God we serve.
- ✓ In the Kingdom, excellence is a lifestyle, not an occasional effort.

Application:

- ✓ Audit customer service, presentation, and product quality—is it worthy of God?
- ✓ Include "Excellence as unto the Lord" in your staff training and onboarding.
- ✓ Avoid shortcuts that compromise quality or truth.
- ✓ Use peer reviews or external evaluations to ensure high standards.
- ✓ Celebrate teams or employees who consistently model excellence.

WEEK 8:
Seek Wisdom, Not Just Knowledge

Scripture:
"If any of you lacks wisdom, you should ask God, who gives generously to all without finding fault, and it will be given to you." – **James 1:5 (NIV)**

Reflection:

- ✓ Knowledge fills your head; wisdom guides your decisions. The marketplace is full of educated fools.
- ✓ God's wisdom surpasses data, trends, and analysis—it discerns hidden motives and sees the unseen.
- ✓ Wise leaders listen more than they speak and seek the Spirit's direction even in everyday decisions.
- ✓ True wisdom values eternal impact over temporary gain.
- ✓ A wise leader seeks input from God first, people second.

Application:

- ✓ Start daily with a prayer for wisdom—especially before meetings or deals.
- ✓ Hold "Wisdom Breaks" with senior teams to slow down, reflect, and recalibrate.
- ✓ Encourage decision logs: What wisdom from Scripture influenced a business move?
- ✓ Train leaders to seek counsel and not rush into decisions under pressure.
- ✓ Avoid glorifying quick, reactive decisions—highlight those born of prayerful wisdom.

WEEK 9:
Be a Giver, Not Just a Taker

Scripture:
"A generous person will prosper; whoever refreshes others will be refreshed." – **Proverbs 11:25 (NIV)**

Reflection:

- ✓ God's economy works differently—blessing flows not through hoarding but giving.
- ✓ Generosity creates open-handed leaders who don't operate from fear but faith.
- ✓ Generous businesses often become trusted brands—people trust those who give without strings.
- ✓ Giving can be financial, but also includes time, mentorship, training, and encouragement.
- ✓ God notices and rewards givers—both now and eternally.

Application:

- ✓ Create a company "generosity initiative" that supports a cause or community need.
- ✓ Provide scholarships or mentorships for underprivileged entrepreneurs or interns.
- ✓ Build a culture of giving by encouraging employees to volunteer or donate.
- ✓ Set a percentage of profits aside for Kingdom work or social impact projects.
- ✓ Teach teams to go the "extra mile" for clients—not for gain, but to give.

WEEK 10:
Guard Against Pride

Scripture:
"Pride goes before destruction, a haughty spirit before a fall." – **Proverbs 16:18 (NIV)**

Reflection:

- ✓ Pride makes leaders unteachable, unreachable, and ultimately, unaccountable.
- ✓ Success is a greater test than failure—it often tempts us to take the glory.
- ✓ Humility invites God's favor; pride invites His opposition (James 4:6).
- ✓ Pride isolates leaders; humility builds community and trust.
- ✓ A proud leader builds a castle; a humble one builds a Kingdom.

Application:

- ✓ Regularly credit God publicly for success—during meetings, interviews, and reports.
- ✓ Invite anonymous feedback from staff to check for blind spots.
- ✓ Surround yourself with people who will tell you the truth—not flatter you.
- ✓ In times of praise or recognition, defer the glory to God and the team.
- ✓ Journal every major achievement and record how God was involved.

WEEK 11:
Lead to Serve, Not to Rule

Scripture:
"Whoever wants to become great among you must be your servant, and whoever wants to be first must be your slave—just as the Son of Man did not come to be served, but to serve..." – **Matthew 20:26–28 (NIV)**

Reflection:

- ✓ Leadership in the Kingdom is defined by service, not status.
- ✓ Servant-leaders prioritize people's well-being over personal comfort.
- ✓ Jesus—the highest leader—demonstrated ultimate humility by washing feet.
- ✓ Serving builds trust, eliminates fear, and fosters loyalty among teams.
- ✓ True authority is earned through humility, not demanded through position.

Application:

- ✓ Begin leadership meetings with the question: "How can we serve our teams better?"
- ✓ Visit lower-level staff regularly to hear concerns firsthand and offer support.
- ✓ Include servant leadership as a key value in the company culture and training.
- ✓ Recognize leaders who serve quietly behind the scenes—not just high performers.
- ✓ Encourage managers to remove roadblocks for their teams instead of creating pressure.

WEEK 12:
Count the Cost Before Committing

Scripture:
"Suppose one of you wants to build a tower. Won't you first sit down and estimate the cost to see if you have enough money to complete it?" – **Luke 14:28 (NIV)**

Reflection:

- ✓ God values planning and preparedness, especially before taking bold steps.
- ✓ Emotional or impulsive decisions can lead to long-term regret in business.
- ✓ Leaders must assess financial, relational, and spiritual implications of every major move.
- ✓ Counting the cost also means evaluating team readiness and resource availability.
- ✓ Faith doesn't mean ignoring risk—it means understanding the cost and trusting God through it.

Application:

- ✓ Before new launches, conduct a thorough resource and feasibility review.
- ✓ Introduce a "pause and plan" checkpoint before greenlighting major initiatives.
- ✓ Involve finance, legal, and operational heads in all strategic decisions early.
- ✓ Reflect on past projects where cost wasn't fully counted—what lessons can be drawn?
- ✓ Avoid romanticizing expansion—grow only when conditions and calling align.

WEEK 13:
Create Order, Not Confusion

Scripture:
"For God is not a God of disorder but of peace…" – **1 Corinthians 14:33 (NIV)**

Reflection:

- ✓ God operates in structure and sequence—chaos is not of His Spirit.
- ✓ Confusion breeds burnout, miscommunication, and inefficiency.
- ✓ A godly business reflects divine clarity in processes, roles, and responsibilities.
- ✓ Order brings peace—people thrive when there is clear direction and structure.
- ✓ Organization and systems are not unspiritual—they are essential for good stewardship.

Application:

- ✓ Revisit and refine your company's workflow systems and SOPs.
- ✓ Create visual org charts and process maps for team clarity.
- ✓ Assign clear responsibilities to avoid role duplication and blame-shifting.
- ✓ Reduce noise in communication—be concise, clear, and confirm understanding.
- ✓ Encourage a clean workspace and digital environment—order promotes peace.

WEEK 14:
Be Faithful in Small Things

Scripture:
"Whoever can be trusted with very little can also be trusted with much…" – **Luke 16:10 (NIV)**

Reflection:

- ✓ Greatness in God's Kingdom begins with faithfulness in little things.
- ✓ Seemingly minor tasks reveal one's true character and diligence.
- ✓ Promotion often comes to those who are consistent behind the scenes.
- ✓ Overlooking the small things can lead to larger failures later.
- ✓ Faithfulness is not measured by visibility but by integrity and consistency.

Application:

- ✓ Review small recurring issues—are they being ignored because they seem "minor"?
- ✓ Publicly acknowledge employees who are consistent in routine tasks.
- ✓ Reinforce diligence in administrative work, customer follow-up, or inventory checks.
- ✓ Include small metrics in performance evaluations to stress consistency.
- ✓ Personally commit to follow through on "small" promises and deadlines.

WEEK 15:
Seek Peace in Conflict

Scripture:
"Blessed are the peacemakers, for they will be called children of God." – **Matthew 5:9 (NIV)**

Reflection:

- ✓ Conflict is inevitable in business, but leaders are called to be peacemakers, not peacekeepers.
- ✓ Peacemaking involves truth, humility, and resolution—not avoidance.
- ✓ A peaceful workplace enhances collaboration, creativity, and productivity.
- ✓ God blesses those who resolve issues with love, fairness, and firmness.
- ✓ Leaders who escalate tension for control damage the long-term culture of the business.

Application:

- ✓ Train department heads in biblical conflict resolution and healthy confrontation.
- ✓ Create open-door policies that allow early surfacing of tension.
- ✓ Model calm, reasoned responses in high-pressure meetings.
- ✓ Do not allow gossip or slander—deal with it firmly and biblically.
- ✓ Establish protocols for reconciliation that reflect Matthew 18:15–17.

WEEK 16:
Lead by Example, Not Just by Words

Scripture:
"Set an example for the believers in speech, in conduct, in love, in faith and in purity." – **1 Timothy 4:12b (NIV)**

Reflection:

- ✓ Leadership is not about issuing commands—it's about modeling what you expect.
- ✓ Teams imitate what leaders do, not just what they say.
- ✓ A consistent, Christlike example inspires excellence, integrity, and accountability.
- ✓ Hypocrisy in leadership is a quick way to erode respect and morale.
- ✓ A godly leader lives a life of transparency, humility, and boldness in doing right.

Application:

- ✓ Examine your daily habits—are you modeling punctuality, diligence, and honor?
- ✓ Start meetings with a tone of humility and integrity—avoid venting or gossiping.
- ✓ Be the first to apologize when you're wrong. It sets the tone for humility.
- ✓ Uphold standards privately and publicly. Never expect what you won't practice.
- ✓ Let employees see your walk of faith—not just on Sundays, but in decisions and ethics.

WEEK 17: Manage Finances with Righteousness

Scripture:
"Dishonest money dwindles away, but whoever gathers money little by little makes it grow." – **Proverbs 13:11 (NIV)**

Reflection:

- ✓ God watches how we handle money—it reflects our values and priorities.
- ✓ Quick gains through unethical means may bring temporary success but result in long-term loss.
- ✓ God honors those who grow wealth through diligence, honesty, and stewardship.
- ✓ Financial integrity builds reputation and opens doors for Kingdom influence.
- ✓ Budgeting, tracking, and disciplined saving reflect wisdom—not stinginess.

Application:

- ✓ Audit income sources and expenses regularly—ensure transparency and legality.
- ✓ Train your finance team in both professional ethics and biblical principles.
- ✓ Avoid exaggeration in profit reports or forecasts—honesty wins long-term trust.
- ✓ Honor contracts, pay debts promptly, and give generously.

- ✓ Build a reserve fund—not just for emergencies, but as a principle of wise stewardship.

WEEK 18:
Serve the Customer with a Christlike Heart

Scripture:
"So in everything, do to others what you would have them do to you..." – **Matthew 7:12 (NIV)**

Reflection:

- ✓ Your clients and customers are people, not profit points—treat them as Christ would.
- ✓ The Golden Rule applies to all interactions—pricing, service, follow-up, and complaints.
- ✓ Service excellence reflects a heart of love, honor, and respect.
- ✓ When we serve well, we open doors for witness, loyalty, and long-term impact.
- ✓ God honors those who choose integrity and kindness, even when it's not convenient.

Application:

- ✓ Review your customer touchpoints—do they reflect dignity and care?
- ✓ Build a feedback mechanism to learn from clients and continually improve.
- ✓ Equip front-line staff to embody Christlike values—patience, truth, helpfulness.
- ✓ Go beyond expectations—especially with those who can't "give back."
- ✓ Never sacrifice customer trust for short-term financial gains.

WEEK 19:
Be Discerning in Partnerships

Scripture:
"Do not be yoked together with unbelievers. For what do righteousness and wickedness have in common?"
– 2 Corinthians 6:14 (NIV)

Reflection:

- ✓ Business partnerships are like yokes—they align you in direction and burden.
- ✓ Unequally yoked partnerships can compromise your values and testimony.
- ✓ Discernment is not fear; it's obedience. God protects us through wise alignment.
- ✓ Be slow to enter into deals—especially when values are unclear or compromised.
- ✓ Kingdom-minded leaders prioritize alignment over opportunity.

Application:

- ✓ Before forming a partnership, assess value alignment—not just profitability.
- ✓ Set up vetting systems and legal counsel rooted in biblical ethics.
- ✓ Don't be afraid to walk away from high-paying deals if the values clash.
- ✓ Pray over all potential alliances—invite spiritual counsel into these decisions.
- ✓ Maintain clarity in agreements—remove ambiguity that might invite dishonor later.

WEEK 20:
Honor the Sabbath and Prioritize Rest

Scripture:
"Remember the Sabbath day by keeping it holy… Six days you shall labor, but the seventh day is a sabbath to the Lord your God." – **Exodus 20:8–10a (NIV)**

Reflection:

- ✓ Rest is not laziness—it is obedience to God's rhythm of life.
- ✓ Burnout is often a result of disobedience disguised as ambition.
- ✓ Sabbath creates space to worship, refresh, reflect, and realign.
- ✓ Leaders who rest show trust in God, not just in their effort or systems.
- ✓ Your team follows your example—if you never pause, neither will they.

Application:

- ✓ Block out your weekly Sabbath—no emails, no urgent tasks. Guard it fiercely.
- ✓ Teach your leadership team the biblical value of rest and refreshment.
- ✓ Schedule business calendars to include rest periods between peak projects.
- ✓ Encourage employees to take vacations and Sabbath pauses seriously.
- ✓ Use your Sabbath to reconnect with family, the Word, and God's voice.

WEEK 21:
Grow Where You Are Planted

Scripture:
"They will be like a tree planted by the water that sends out its roots by the stream…"
– **Jeremiah 17:8a (NIV)**

Reflection:

- ✓ God often calls us to grow right where we are, before moving us forward.
- ✓ Chasing opportunity over faithfulness leads to instability and restlessness.
- ✓ Growth happens through deep roots, not constant uprooting.
- ✓ When your business is aligned with God, it will flourish in season—even in dry times.
- ✓ Your location, team, or market may seem small—but faithfulness makes it fruitful.

Application:

- ✓ Resist the urge to constantly compare your business to others—focus on where God has placed you.
- ✓ Invest in your current staff, systems, and resources—strengthen what you have.
- ✓ Teach your team to value deep work and long-term commitment.
- ✓ If tempted to move, ask: Is this God's leading or my impatience?
- ✓ Celebrate "small wins" as signs of rooted growth, not insignificance.

WEEK 22:
Communicate Truth with Grace

Scripture:
"Instead, speaking the truth in love, we will grow to become in every respect the mature body…" – **Ephesians 4:15 (NIV)**

Reflection:

- ✓ Truth without love is harsh; love without truth is compromise—Kingdom leadership requires both.
- ✓ Clear, honest, and gracious communication builds a strong, healthy culture.
- ✓ Avoiding truth to maintain comfort is short-sighted and unloving.
- ✓ Confrontation is often necessary—but must be done in humility and compassion.
- ✓ How we communicate reflects who we follow—Christ, the embodiment of grace and truth.

Application:

- ✓ Train your leaders in giving feedback that uplifts while correcting.
- ✓ Practice "truth in love" conversations—don't delay important issues out of fear.
- ✓ Address team misunderstandings early and directly—don't allow resentment to build.
- ✓ Avoid sarcasm, passive-aggressiveness, or emotional outbursts—these damage trust.
- ✓ Make space for employees to speak truth back to leadership respectfully.

WEEK 23:
Wait for God's Timing

Scripture:
"There is a time for everything, and a season for every activity under the heavens..."
– **Ecclesiastes 3:1 (NIV)**

Reflection:

- ✓ Timing is just as important as vision. A great idea launched prematurely can fail.
- ✓ God's delays are not denials—they are developments in disguise.
- ✓ The marketplace may pressure speed, but the Kingdom values process.
- ✓ Waiting seasons strengthen discernment, deepen prayer, and test motives.
- ✓ Rushing may bypass God's best—peace is often the indicator of divine timing.

Application:

- ✓ Revisit major decisions that seem delayed—could God be protecting or preparing you?
- ✓ Discern between market urgency and Holy Spirit prompting.
- ✓ Avoid making rushed decisions in times of fear, fatigue, or frustration.
- ✓ Use waiting periods for deeper strategy, training, or prayer—not idle worry.
- ✓ Encourage your team: "We move when God says go—not just when the world demands it."

WEEK 24:
Prepare for Succession and Legacy

Scripture:
"Now Joshua son of Nun was filled with the spirit of wisdom because Moses had laid his hands on him..."
– **Deuteronomy 34:9 (NIV)**

Reflection:

- ✓ Great leaders think beyond themselves—they prepare successors, not just successors-in-title.
- ✓ Moses' final act was empowering Joshua—a leader's true legacy is seen in who follows.
- ✓ Succession should not be a reaction to crisis, but a deliberate process of impartation.
- ✓ God-honoring businesses prioritize continuity of values, not just structure.
- ✓ If your leadership ends today, does your vision outlive you?

Application:

- ✓ Identify and invest in emerging leaders—both in skill and spiritual grounding.
- ✓ Create mentorship pipelines that transmit wisdom, not just roles.
- ✓ Begin documenting vision, core values, and strategic history early.
- ✓ Discuss succession openly at the board level—don't avoid it out of discomfort.
- ✓ Pray intentionally over who will carry your legacy forward.

WEEK 25:
Stay Humble in Success

Scripture:
"Humble yourselves before the Lord, and He will lift you up." – **James 4:10 (NIV)**

Reflection:

- ✓ Success is a test of character—will you glorify God or yourself?
- ✓ Humility acknowledges that everything comes from God, not merely your effort or strategy.
- ✓ Pride shuts the door to wisdom and correction; humility keeps it open.
- ✓ God honors the lowly and resists the proud—even in boardrooms and balance sheets.
- ✓ True success is not measured by status, but by how low you bow before the Lord.

Application:

- ✓ Give public credit to God for every milestone or achievement.
- ✓ Avoid titles, awards, or accolades becoming your identity—stay grounded in service.
- ✓ Invite trusted voices to speak into your blind spots—don't surround yourself with yes-men.
- ✓ Reflect regularly on where God brought you from.
- ✓ Use success as a platform for generosity and testimony, not self-glory.

WEEK 26:
Choose Righteousness Over Profit

Scripture:
"Better a little with righteousness than much gain with injustice." – **Proverbs 16:8 (NIV)**

Reflection:

- ✓ God's economy prioritizes righteousness over riches—doing what's right over what's lucrative.
- ✓ Short-term profits made through questionable means will eventually attract loss—financial or spiritual.
- ✓ Obedience to God's standards may cost money in the short run, but yields peace and favor in the long run.
- ✓ The temptation to compromise often comes when stakes are high—that's when faith must rise higher.
- ✓ Kingdom business leaders are called to walk the narrow path, even in competitive markets.

Application:

- ✓ Audit your pricing, sourcing, vendor partnerships, and sales practices—is there anything unjust?
- ✓ Create a non-negotiable values list for decision-making—even under financial pressure.
- ✓ Train your team to refuse shady deals, no matter the gain.

- ✓ Share testimonies of when your business chose right over rich—and how God honored it.
- ✓ Pray before every major contract: “Lord, help me choose righteousness even if it costs.”

WEEK 27:
Stand Firm in Adversity

Scripture:
"Therefore put on the full armor of God, so that when the day of evil comes, you may be able to stand your ground..." – **Ephesians 6:13 (NIV)**

Reflection:

- ✓ Adversity is inevitable in business—but it's not meant to destroy you; it's meant to develop you.
- ✓ Spiritual battles often take the form of economic pressure, leadership conflict, or temptation to quit.
- ✓ God equips leaders to stand firm—not by their strength, but through His armor (truth, faith, righteousness, etc.).
- ✓ Stability in storms earns trust from teams, clients, and observers—it reflects the peace of God.
- ✓ Leaders must choose faith over fear and perseverance over panic.

Application:

- ✓ Begin each day with prayer and a "spiritual armor" check (Eph. 6:10–18).
- ✓ Encourage staff during difficult seasons with hope and practical wisdom.
- ✓ Avoid reactive decision-making during crises—pause, pray, and consult.
- ✓ Build a culture where hardship is met with resilience, not retreat.

- ✓ Keep a “God’s faithfulness file”—a written reminder of past battles He helped you win.

WEEK 28:
Create an Atmosphere of Honor

Scripture:
"Be devoted to one another in love. Honor one another above yourselves." – **Romans 12:10 (NIV)**

Reflection:

- ✓ Honor is the spiritual currency of Kingdom relationships—it unlocks influence and trust.
- ✓ Workplaces that practice honor become magnets for loyalty, creativity, and collaboration.
- ✓ Honoring others is not flattery—it's recognizing God's value in every person.
- ✓ Conflict is reduced where honor is practiced consistently, even in disagreements.
- ✓ The way leaders speak about and treat their people sets the tone for the entire culture.

Application:

- ✓ Publicly affirm team members for effort, not just results.
- ✓ Eliminate gossip and slander—make it a zero-tolerance culture.
- ✓ Greet even the lowest-level staff with respect and presence.
- ✓ Honor clients, vendors, and competitors by being fair and ethical in dealings.
- ✓ Incorporate "honor reports" in team meetings—shout-outs for excellence and integrity.

WEEK 29:
Obedience Over Outcome

Scripture:
"To obey is better than sacrifice, and to heed is better than the fat of rams." – **1 Samuel 15:22 (NIV)**

Reflection:

- ✓ God is more interested in your obedience than your performance metrics.
- ✓ Sacrificing time, money, or effort doesn't please God if disobedience is in the foundation.
- ✓ Outcomes don't validate methods—even "successful" results can be outside God's will.
- ✓ Obedience doesn't always make earthly sense—but it aligns us with heavenly wisdom.
- ✓ When leaders choose obedience, they open doors for divine intervention and unexpected provision.

Application:

- ✓ Before major launches or hires, ask: "Is this God's will or just good strategy?"
- ✓ Obey God's promptings even when they feel risky—He sees beyond the immediate.
- ✓ Share obedience testimonies in leadership devotionals to build faith.
- ✓ If something is working but contradicts biblical values—shut it down.
- ✓ Remind yourself daily: "I'm called to be obedient, not just effective."

WEEK 30:
Speak with Integrity

Scripture:
"The words of the reckless pierce like swords, but the tongue of the wise brings healing." – **Proverbs 12:18 (NIV)**

Reflection:

- ✓ Leaders' words shape culture, morale, and direction—careless words can destroy what took years to build.
- ✓ Speech that aligns with God's truth builds trust and fosters healing.
- ✓ Integrity in speech includes promises, feedback, emails, and even silence.
- ✓ A leader's credibility is often measured not just by performance—but by the truthfulness of their word.
- ✓ Wise communication requires discipline, especially in emotionally charged moments.

Application:

- ✓ Avoid exaggeration, overpromising, or flattery in leadership communication.
- ✓ Follow through on all verbal commitments—no matter how small.
- ✓ Implement a culture of "clean speech"—truth spoken in kindness and clarity.
- ✓ Record and reflect on team interactions—are your words building or bruising?
- ✓ Teach leaders to speak life over people and projects—no careless negativity.

WEEK 31:
Embrace God-Inspired Innovation

Scripture:
"See, I am doing a new thing! Now it springs up; do you not perceive it?" – **Isaiah 43:19 (NIV)**

Reflection:

- ✓ God is a Creator and Innovator—He loves doing new things through His people.
- ✓ Innovation in business must be Spirit-led, not just trend-driven.
- ✓ God's creativity often breaks conventional molds to birth extraordinary results.
- ✓ Staying stuck in "the way things have always been done" can hinder divine growth.
- ✓ Leaders should be open to God's voice in strategy, product design, marketing, and systems.

Application:

- ✓ Set aside time monthly to pray for divine creativity in business areas.
- ✓ Encourage a company culture that rewards godly innovation and risk-taking.
- ✓ Don't dismiss new ideas just because they're unfamiliar—discern them prayerfully.
- ✓ Invite cross-functional brainstorming under the theme: "What's the 'new thing' God may want here?"
- ✓ Document and testify how God-inspired ideas led to breakthroughs.

WEEK 32:
Be Led by the Spirit, Not Just the Market

Scripture:
"Since we live by the Spirit, let us keep in step with the Spirit." – **Galatians 5:25 (NIV)**

Reflection:

- ✓ Market research is helpful, but the Holy Spirit is the greatest strategist.
- ✓ Spirit-led leaders move at God's pace, not the market's pressure.
- ✓ Keeping in step with the Spirit involves listening, waiting, and obeying—even when others don't understand.
- ✓ There will be times when divine direction contradicts logic—but brings supernatural results.
- ✓ You're not just a CEO—you're a Spirit-filled ambassador of God's Kingdom in the marketplace.

Application:

- ✓ Begin strategic meetings with dedicated prayer and Scripture meditation.
- ✓ Journal spiritual impressions and cross-reference them with Scripture and wise counsel.
- ✓ Don't ignore "checks in the spirit" just because an opportunity looks lucrative.
- ✓ Build a leadership habit of asking: "What is the Spirit saying about this?"

- ✓ Celebrate and document stories of when following the Spirit paid off—even when it didn't make sense initially.

WEEK 33:
Hire Character, Train Skills

Scripture:
"Choose men of good reputation, full of the Spirit and of wisdom, whom we may put in charge…" – **Acts 6:3 (NASB)**

Reflection:

- ✓ God's hiring model prioritizes character and spiritual depth over just competence.
- ✓ A skilled team member with poor values can undo more than they build.
- ✓ Character drives loyalty, accountability, and unity—essential in a thriving business.
- ✓ Skills can be developed, but integrity must be discerned and nurtured.
- ✓ You're not just building a company—you're building a culture and testimony.

Application:

- ✓ Revamp interview processes to assess values, not just technical ability.
- ✓ Ask character-revealing questions: "Tell me about a time you admitted failure."
- ✓ Pray over each key hire; involve godly advisors if possible.
- ✓ Check references for more than job performance—ask about work ethic, honesty, and teamwork.
- ✓ Develop your HR strategy around mentoring and discipling, not just managing.

WEEK 34:
Handle Wealth with Reverence

Scripture:

"Command those who are rich… not to be arrogant nor to put their hope in wealth… but to put their hope in God…" – **1 Timothy 6:17 (NIV)**

Reflection:

- ✓ Wealth is a tool, not a trophy—it must be handled with responsibility and humility.
- ✓ God entrusts financial success so it can be used for eternal impact, not just comfort.
- ✓ Riches can easily become an idol if we shift our trust from the Provider to the provision.
- ✓ Every financial decision is a spiritual decision—does it reflect God's values?
- ✓ Humility, gratitude, and generosity must rise alongside profit and scale.

Application:

- ✓ Practice regular financial giving—tithes, offerings, and Kingdom support.
- ✓ Avoid placing hope in forecasts, balance sheets, or reserves—keep trust anchored in God.
- ✓ Build in accountability for major financial decisions—invite both business and spiritual counsel.
- ✓ Create a corporate generosity initiative tied to your mission and biblical values.
- ✓ Frequently declare and remind your team: "This business belongs to God."

WEEK 35:
Don't Find Your Identity in the Title

Scripture:
"Do not rejoice that the spirits submit to you, but rejoice that your names are written in heaven." – **Luke 10:20 (NIV)**

Reflection:

- ✓ Success, titles, and accolades are fleeting—your true identity is found in Christ.
- ✓ Leadership is a calling, not a crown—it doesn't define your worth.
- ✓ When identity is tied to role or reputation, any failure or change becomes personal.
- ✓ Security in Christ allows you to lead with confidence without ego or comparison.
- ✓ Even Jesus laid down His reputation to fulfill His purpose—so must we.

Application:

- ✓ Regularly reaffirm who you are in Christ: loved, called, and chosen—not just "CEO" or "Founder."
- ✓ Hold your role loosely, but your relationship with God tightly.
- ✓ Mentor younger leaders to avoid the trap of self-worth tied to titles or performance.
- ✓ Make room for feedback and correction—without defensiveness.
- ✓ Step into leadership spaces with humility and the mindset of a servant, not a star.

WEEK 36:
Influence with Integrity

Scripture:
"Let your light shine before others, that they may see your good deeds and glorify your Father in heaven."
– **Matthew 5:16 (NIV)**

Reflection:

- ✓ Your business is a platform of influence, not just for profit, but for Kingdom witness.
- ✓ Influence without integrity is manipulation; influence with integrity is ministry.
- ✓ People are always watching—your conduct may draw them toward or away from Christ.
- ✓ The world respects excellence, but it remembers authenticity and moral courage.
- ✓ Let your business model, customer care, and leadership point upward, not inward.

Application:

- ✓ Establish a "Kingdom Impact" goal alongside profit targets—how are you influencing lives?
- ✓ Review advertising and communication—do they reflect biblical values or worldly hype?
- ✓ Choose suppliers, partners, and clients who align with your integrity, even if it costs more.
- ✓ Train staff to understand their influence—every call, email, and decision is a witness.
- ✓ Model repentance and humility publicly when mistakes are made—it enhances influence, not weakens it.

WEEK 37:
Stay Excellent Under Pressure

Scripture:
"And let us not grow weary in doing good, for at the proper time we will reap a harvest if we do not give up." – **Galatians 6:9 (NIV)**

Reflection:

- ✓ Pressure is part of leadership, but your response reveals your maturity.
- ✓ Excellence is not seasonal—it's a standard, even in storms.
- ✓ Consistency under stress builds trust, stability, and Kingdom witness.
- ✓ Your team will mimic your response to pressure—panic or poise.
- ✓ God strengthens those who press on in obedience, even when it's difficult.

Application:

- ✓ Establish stress management practices rooted in faith—Scripture reading, prayer breaks, worship moments.
- ✓ Don't lower ethical standards to meet deadlines—stay committed to quality and righteousness.
- ✓ Acknowledge pressure without letting it define the environment—speak peace, not panic.
- ✓ Affirm your team's efforts and endurance during crunch times.
- ✓ Reflect after high-pressure seasons: What did God teach? What can be improved?

WEEK 38:
Build with the Future in Mind

Scripture:
"A good person leaves an inheritance for their children's children..." – **Proverbs 13:22a (NIV)**

Reflection:

- ✓ Short-term wins are not the goal—legacy is.
- ✓ Businesses rooted in Kingdom principles don't just think about the next quarter—but the next generation.
- ✓ Leaving a legacy includes faith, values, leadership succession, and generosity.
- ✓ If your business vanished today, would its spiritual and social impact be remembered?
- ✓ God-honoring leaders plant seeds today that bear fruit in eternity.

Application:

- ✓ Write a "Business Legacy Statement" that reflects both mission and ministry goals.
- ✓ Create long-term value—invest in people, not just products.
- ✓ Document Kingdom practices so future leaders continue the vision.
- ✓ Educate your children, mentees, or successors in both business skills and biblical convictions.
- ✓ Celebrate 10-, 15-, and 25-year goals that go beyond profit to purpose.

WEEK 39:
Discipline Brings Dominion

Scripture:
"No discipline seems pleasant at the time, but painful. Later on, however, it produces a harvest of righteousness and peace..." – **Hebrews 12:11 (NIV)**

Reflection:

- ✓ Discipline is the bridge between vision and reality—it's what sustains excellence.
- ✓ God trains those He loves—discipline is not punishment, it's preparation.
- ✓ Consistency in small things unlocks influence in big things.
- ✓ Emotional decisions sabotage progress; disciplined choices bring dominion.
- ✓ Every business that thrives has systems—and systems require discipline.

Application:

- ✓ Create daily and weekly disciplines for prayer, planning, and progress review.
- ✓ Coach your team to set habits and routines that align with long-term goals.
- ✓ Review areas where emotions, laziness, or fear have replaced order—reset them.
- ✓ Reward consistency, not just performance.
- ✓ Remind yourself that godly discipline isn't legalism—it's leadership.

WEEK 40:
Seek Wise Counsel Before You Decide

Scripture:
"Plans fail for lack of counsel, but with many advisers they succeed." – **Proverbs 15:22 (NIV)**

Reflection:

- ✓ God uses people—mentors, spiritual advisors, and wise friends—to guide your path.
- ✓ Pride resists counsel; humility seeks it out.
- ✓ Major decisions made in isolation often result in costly mistakes.
- ✓ Surrounding yourself with godly, diverse counsel strengthens both strategy and discernment.
- ✓ Seeking input doesn't mean indecision—it reflects maturity.

Application:

- ✓ Build a trusted "wisdom circle" that includes spiritual mentors, business experts, and intercessors.
- ✓ Before making major moves (acquisitions, hires, expansion), consult with them.
- ✓ Create a culture where your team is encouraged to seek feedback, not hide struggles.
- ✓ Record the input received and how it influenced key decisions.
- ✓ Pray over counsel to discern what's of God, then act with faith and confidence.

WEEK 41:
Guard the Unity of Your Team

Scripture:
"Make every effort to keep the unity of the Spirit through the bond of peace." – **Ephesians 4:3 (NIV)**

Reflection:

- ✓ Unity is a supernatural force—when present, it attracts God's blessing (Psalm 133).
- ✓ Division in the workplace is not just a leadership issue—it's a spiritual threat.
- ✓ Gossip, comparison, and offense are weapons of disunity that must be uprooted early.
- ✓ Unity doesn't mean uniformity—diverse voices aligned in purpose create powerful teams.
- ✓ The enemy targets unity because he knows its power—wise leaders protect it fiercely.

Application:

- ✓ Set clear values for communication and team conduct—make honor non-negotiable.
- ✓ Address conflict early with biblical conflict-resolution practices (see Matthew 18:15–17).
- ✓ Celebrate team wins rather than individual glory—build a "we" culture.
- ✓ Conduct regular check-ins for team health and relational integrity.
- ✓ Teach and model forgiveness, empathy, and listening as leadership tools.

WEEK 42:
Steward What You've Been Given

Scripture:
"Each of you should use whatever gift you have received to serve others, as faithful stewards of God's grace…" – **1 Peter 4:10 (NIV)**

Reflection:

- ✓ God is the true Owner—we are stewards of people, resources, and influence.
- ✓ Stewardship is not just about money—it includes time, talents, opportunities, and relationships.
- ✓ Faithful stewards multiply what is given, not just maintain it.
- ✓ Wastefulness, negligence, and entitlement are signs of poor stewardship.
- ✓ God entrusts more to those who are faithful with little (Luke 16:10).

Application:

- ✓ Conduct quarterly audits—not just of finances, but of time, talents, and team health.
- ✓ Invest in the development of people—not just in tools or assets.
- ✓ Repurpose unused or underutilized resources—nothing should lie dormant.
- ✓ Train your team in the "why" of stewardship—not just efficiency, but faithfulness.
- ✓ Pray over all you manage: "Lord, help me multiply and honor what You've entrusted."

WEEK 43:
Handle Criticism with Grace

Scripture:
"A gentle answer turns away wrath, but a harsh word stirs up anger." – **Proverbs 15:1 (NIV)**

Reflection:

- ✓ Criticism is inevitable for leaders—but how you respond defines your maturity.
- ✓ Not all criticism is harmful; some is God's tool for growth and refinement.
- ✓ Defensive or angry responses damage your witness and team trust.
- ✓ A gentle answer—even in the face of unfair critique—diffuses tension and invites respect.
- ✓ Leaders must distinguish between correction from God and attack from the enemy.

Application:

- ✓ Pause before responding to critique—ask: "Is this true? Is it helpful? Is it God?"
- ✓ Thank sincere critics—even if their tone was poor; you'll grow from their insight.
- ✓ Protect your spirit from bitterness—pray for those who offend you.
- ✓ Coach your team to give and receive feedback graciously and biblically.
- ✓ Journal constructive criticism and review what God might be teaching you through it.

WEEK 44:
Maintain Vision Beyond the Natural

Scripture:
"For we live by faith, not by sight." – **2 Corinthians 5:7 (NIV)**

Reflection:

- ✓ Natural circumstances must never dictate spiritual leadership—faith sees the unseen.
- ✓ Challenges are real, but God's promises are greater—don't lose your spiritual vision.
- ✓ Visionaries must often stand alone in seasons where others see only limitation.
- ✓ God honors faith that clings to His Word despite physical evidence.
- ✓ Your spiritual sight will guide your business through seasons of drought into harvest.

Application:

- ✓ Keep a "Vision Wall" or journal where promises from God are visible and reviewed often.
- ✓ Declare Scripture over your business—speak God's Word, not just market reality.
- ✓ Train yourself and your team to make decisions in prayer, not fear.
- ✓ Celebrate testimonies where faith led to breakthrough—build collective memory.
- ✓ Surround yourself with faith-filled people who can help you "see" when you feel blind.

WEEK 45:
Trust God in Uncertainty

Scripture:
"Trust in the Lord with all your heart and lean not on your own understanding…" – **Proverbs 3:5 (NIV)**

Reflection:

- ✓ Uncertainty is part of life—but faith anchors you to a steady God.
- ✓ Trust doesn't mean you know every outcome—it means you know the One who does.
- ✓ Leaning on your own logic will eventually lead to fear or burnout.
- ✓ God often withholds clarity to build dependence, not confusion.
- ✓ Your deepest peace will come not from having answers—but from trusting God's hand.

Application:

- ✓ Practice surrender in prayer daily—"Lord, I trust You more than my plan."
- ✓ Avoid rushing into decisions to escape discomfort—wait for God's timing.
- ✓ Journal your uncertainties—and beside each, write a promise from God.
- ✓ Encourage your team to bring concerns to God first, not last.
- ✓ Read stories of biblical leaders (Abraham, Joseph, Esther) who thrived through uncertainty.

WEEK 46:
Cultivate a Spirit of Gratitude

Scripture:
"Give thanks in all circumstances; for this is God's will for you in Christ Jesus." – **1 Thessalonians 5:18 (NIV)**

Reflection:

- ✓ Gratitude is not based on circumstances—it's an attitude of the heart rooted in trust.
- ✓ Thankfulness shifts your focus from lack to abundance, and from pressure to presence.
- ✓ Grateful leaders inspire joy, resilience, and unity in their teams.
- ✓ Complaining leaders foster fear and discontentment—gratitude is leadership oxygen.
- ✓ Gratitude attracts the favor of God and opens your eyes to opportunities already around you.

Application:

- ✓ Begin every team meeting or workday with a moment of thanksgiving.
- ✓ Keep a "Gratitude Log" to record business breakthroughs, big or small.
- ✓ Send regular appreciation messages to staff, clients, and vendors.
- ✓ Celebrate progress as much as completion—thank God and your team.
- ✓ Practice thanking God in advance for things you're trusting Him to do.

WEEK 47:
Finish What You Start

Scripture:
"Finishing is better than starting. Patience is better than pride." – **Ecclesiastes 7:8 (NLT)**

Reflection:

- ✓ Many start with excitement, but few finish with excellence.
- ✓ Finishing strong requires patience, focus, and a deep commitment to purpose.
- ✓ The enemy often attacks at the edge of breakthrough—stay the course.
- ✓ Half-built towers and abandoned visions reflect poorly on God's ambassadors.
- ✓ God is a Finisher—He who began the work in you is faithful to complete it (Phil. 1:6).

Application:

- ✓ Revisit unfinished projects—ask God which to revive, release, or complete.
- ✓ Build a team culture that honors deadlines and values completion.
- ✓ Break large goals into weekly "finishable" actions.
- ✓ Celebrate completed initiatives to set a finish-strong culture.
- ✓ Let your excellence in finishing testify to the faithfulness of God.

WEEK 48:
Build a Prayer-Driven Business

Scripture:
"Unless the Lord builds the house, the builders labor in vain." – **Psalm 127:1a (NIV)**

Reflection:

- ✓ Every great business decision should begin and end with prayer.
- ✓ Prayer invites God's wisdom, protection, timing, and provision.
- ✓ Without prayer, we rely on human logic—but with it, we receive divine strategy.
- ✓ A prayer-driven business acknowledges God as CEO and source.
- ✓ Prayer aligns you with Kingdom priorities and keeps pride in check.

Application:

- ✓ Dedicate time weekly for prayer over key departments and projects.
- ✓ Create prayer groups within your team—cover business goals in intercession.
- ✓ Start meetings with short moments of Scripture and prayer.
- ✓ Ask for discernment before signing any contract or partnership.
- ✓ Keep a "Prayer Wall" with answered prayers to remind your team of God's hand.

WEEK 49:
Carry the Weight of Responsibility with Grace

Scripture:
"To whom much is given, much will be required." –
Luke 12:48b (NLT)

Reflection:

- ✓ Leadership is not a privilege—it's a sacred responsibility entrusted by God.
- ✓ The higher your position, the deeper your dependence on God's grace must be.
- ✓ Avoid the temptation to control everything—grace, not grit, sustains your leadership.
- ✓ Carrying the weight with grace means delegating wisely, leading humbly, and trusting constantly.
- ✓ God does not call you to bear the load alone—He equips those He appoints.

Application:

- ✓ Ask God daily for wisdom to handle leadership responsibility with balance and peace.
- ✓ Share leadership burdens with a core team—don't walk alone.
- ✓ Delegate, but never abdicate—stay connected while empowering others.
- ✓ Invite accountability to stay grounded and godly.
- ✓ Make space for sabbath and rest—rest is a leadership discipline, not a luxury.

WEEK 50:
Operate from Purpose, Not Pressure

Scripture:
"But I have raised you up for this very purpose…" –
Exodus 9:16 (NIV)

Reflection:

- ✓ You were called to lead with purpose, not react to pressure.
- ✓ Pressure produces burnout; purpose fuels perseverance.
- ✓ God's purpose brings clarity during chaos and direction in decisions.
- ✓ When you lead from purpose, distractions lose their power.
- ✓ Purpose-driven leaders inspire legacy, not just productivity.

Application:

- ✓ Define and review your business's God-given purpose—write it out and share it often.
- ✓ Say no to opportunities that dilute or distract from your purpose.
- ✓ Refocus your goals around what matters eternally, not just quarterly.
- ✓ In moments of overwhelm, pause and ask: "What is the purpose here?"
- ✓ Align hiring, branding, and partnerships with your higher mission.

WEEK 51:
Remember the Faithfulness of God

Scripture:
"Because of the Lord's great love we are not consumed, for his compassions never fail. They are new every morning; great is your faithfulness." – **Lamentations 3:22–23 (NIV)**

Reflection:

- ✓ Behind every breakthrough, contract, and milestone stands God's faithfulness.
- ✓ Remembering God's faithfulness fuels hope for the future.
- ✓ A forgetful heart becomes an anxious one—remembrance brings peace.
- ✓ Faithful leaders are rooted in the history of God's provision.
- ✓ Gratitude and testimony make your business a living altar of praise.

Application:

- ✓ Keep a "Faithfulness File"—document God's hand over the business journey.
- ✓ Share testimonies of answered prayer with your team and stakeholders.
- ✓ Reflect annually on how God carried you through challenges.
- ✓ Turn your year-end review into a time of thanksgiving and worship.
- ✓ Publicly declare: "This business is a testament to the faithfulness of God."

WEEK 52:
Leave a Kingdom Legacy

Scripture:
"Only what is done for Christ will last." – (Inspired by **1 Corinthians 3:11–15**)

Reflection:

- ✓ Your greatest achievement is not what you build, but what you leave behind for God's glory.
- ✓ Legacy is not about assets—it's about impact, values, and eternal fruit.
- ✓ Kingdom-minded leaders prepare others, not just profits.
- ✓ Your story should outlive you and point others to Jesus.
- ✓ A legacy is not written at the end of your career—it's built daily, decision by decision.

Application:

- ✓ Invest time in mentoring, discipleship, and character building.
- ✓ Evaluate what you want people to say about your business 10 years after you're gone.
- ✓ Create written vision statements and values that reflect eternal purpose.
- ✓ Involve your family and team in building something that matters eternally.
- ✓ Let your final goal be this: "Well done, good and faithful servant."

About the Author
'GERARD ASSEY'

Gerard Assey is a Graduate in Economics, a PGD in Management (HRD) and holds a Doctorate in Leadership. Gerard holds several International Qualifications in Sales, Debt Collection, Training & Teaching, and is a 'Fellow' of the prestigious 'Institute of Sales & Marketing Management'-UK, a Certified NLP Practitioner, a 'Certified Trainer', an 'Accredited Management Teacher-Behavioral Sciences', a 'Certified Competency Facilitator', a 'Certified Management Consultant'- (the International credentials of a professional management consultant, awarded in accordance with global standards of the ICMCI); and a Certification from the University of Michigan in 'Successful Negotiation: Essential Strategies and Skills'

He is also a Member of the 'National Association of Sales Professionals' backed with several years experience in varied industries, both in India and Overseas. He also holds an 'Etiquette Consultant' Certification from the USA (by Sue Fox, Author of Best Seller: 'Business Etiquette for Dummies'. She has trained some of the top celebrities' world over). He was also a recipient of a scholarship for extensive training in Japan on 'Corporate Management for India'.

Gerard Assey is 'Founder & Chief Corporate Trainer' of the Group: **'Citius, Altius, Fortius Unlimited'**- an organization that **celebrated 20 years of Glorious Service** in 2021, focusing on 3 Core Competencies:

People. Performance. Profit; in functional areas of Sales & Marketing, HR & Organizational Development, covering Recruitment, Training & Consultancy!

Having managed organizations with large Sales Forces in India & Overseas, his specialization cover extensive areas of Sales Training (All levels - Presentation, Negotiation, Key/ Strategic Accounts Management & Managerial Skills for all sectors), Bid Proposal/ Capture Planning/ Management Trainings, Retail Sales, Customer Service & Customer Retention Programs, Training for Prevention & Collection of Debt, Self & Personal Development Programs (Time Management, Teamwork & Team Building, Business Etiquette & Personal Grooming, Leadership & Managerial Skills, People Management Skills, Train-the-Trainer etc), including preparation of Custom-designed Business Manuals for Internal (HR, Induction, and Sales etc) & External use (Instruction, User Manuals).

Gerard has successfully conducted over 6460 Trainings & Workshops (as of June '25) all across India, Middle East, Africa, Europe & S.E. Asia. Besides public programs conducted regularly, both in India & Overseas, he has some of the top names as clients whom he services from Single Owners to large Public & Government undertakings, covering all sectors, for their in-house needs.

His website: www.CollectionSkills.com is the only one in this part of the world to be featured in the 'Collections & Credit Risk Magazine-USA' under 'Who's Who in Training' and ranks TOP, along with other websites listed below on most search engines.

Gerard is author of 197 books already (July 2025), all the books being available on all online platforms and outlets as E-books and Paperbacks

A few of our business related books:

1. Bite-sized Bits on Commonsense Management
2. Heart to Heart on Life's Principles'
3. How to become a Successful Manager
4. The Sales Professionals' Master Workbook of S.Y.S.T.E.M.S
5. The Professional Business Email Etiquette Handbook & Guide
6. The Professional Business Video-Conferencing Etiquette Handbook & Guide
7. Professional Presentation Skills
8. Exceptional Customer Service
9. Professional Tele-Marketing Skills
10. Professional Debt Collection Skills
11. The G.R.E.A.T. Sales & Service Workbook
12. Sales Training Advantage for Results (*The Ultimate Sales Training Manual to enable you stand out as a S.T.A.R.*)
13. CEO Daily Planner & Organizer
14. The Sales Professionals' Master Daily Planner
15. The Professional Debt Collector's Master Daily Planner
16. My Daily Planner & Organizer
17. MY EMERGENCY INFORMATION RECORD (Family Emergency & Peace of Mind Planner)
18. The Ultimate Therapist & Counselors Planner and Organizer
19. Building an Ethical Workplace
20. Managing Relationships at Work
21. Managing Business Meetings Effectively
22. Effective Delegation Skills
23. Goal Setting for Success
24. B2B Selling by Email
25. Professional Business Etiquette & Grooming
26. Dining Etiquette & Table Manners
27. Effective Networking Skills
28. Grooming, Etiquette & Manners for Teens, Young Adults & Future Leaders
29. Inter-Personal Skills
30. Get Ready, Get Hired!
31. Selling in a Recession
32. Effective Receivables Management in an Economic Downturn!
33. Real Estate & Property Sales Training
34. Credit Sales & Accounts Receivable Management

35. Selling Skills for Real Estate & Property Advisors
36. Take G.R.E.A.T. C.A.R.E!
37. Spa, Salon & Health Club Selling Skills
38. Selling Travel, Holiday & MICE Services
39. Selling Skills for Spa's, Salons & Health Clubs
40. Retailing in Salons & Spas
41. Selling Holiday, Vacation, Tours & Packages
42. The Power of Sales Referrals
43. Selling Luxury
44. Technical Selling Skills
45. Financial Advisors Sales Training
46. Dealing with Burnout at Work Monopolize Your Markets
47. Selling to Affluent Customers
48. Growing up with Grace
49. Financial Selling Skills
50. *The Effective Manager's Guide: Key Skills to Thrive*
51. From Aspiring to Inspiring: A Guide for New Managers on the Rise
52. The Power of Focus
53. Selling with Integrity: Sell Like Jesus The Perfect Role Model!
54. 31 Habits of Champions: Your 31-Day Journey to Greatness
55. Rejecting Grasshopper Talk: From Grasshopper to Giant-Killer-*Defeating Giants Daily!*
56. Navigate the AI-Powered Future of Bid & Proposals: Up-Skill to Stay Relevant with Alternative Career Paths & Opportunities
57. Hiring Sales Winners
58. Present with Impact
59. Success Unlocked: *Breaking Free from Habits that Hold You Back*
60. Complaints to Cheers, Feedback to Gold: Mastering Complaints Management
61. Thriving Together: *Cultivating Diversity, Equity, and Inclusion*
62. Coaching Skills for Sales Managers
63. Soaring to Success in Business & Leadership: Swifter, Higher, Stronger!
64. From Classroom to Podium: A Student's Guide to Powerful Public Speaking & Presentation Skills
65. Developing Self-Discipline
66. The CEO's 31-Day Power Plan: Unlocking Success through Essential Traits

67. Credibility Matters
68. A Winning Attitude
69. Bid & Proposal Management Using AI
70. Sales Forecasting: A Practical & Proven Guide to Strategic Sales Forecasting
71. Elevate & Energize: *50 Dynamic & Fun Activities for Peak Workplace Morale*
72. 'Sales SOS! Sales on Fire! *30 Days to Conquer Chaos & the Nightmares of Success!'*
73. Mastering Sales Managerial Skills: *Building High-Performing Teams & Driving Exceptional Results*
74. Eagle-Eyed Leadership: Unleashing the Power of 31 Lessons from Eagles
75. The Ultimate Employee Training Guide: *Training Today, Leading Tomorrow*
76. Being More Accountable at Work
77. Creating a Culture of Continuous Improvement
78. Effective Questioning & Listening Skills
79. The Power of Value Selling
80. The Growth Mindset
81. Mastering Professional Help Desk Skills
82. The Power to Lead with Empathy
83. Being Prepared: The Key to Unlocking Success
84. Youthful Spark-Youth Energizers, Activities and Games-Igniting the Fun in Youth
85. Ignite your Motivation for Success
86. Elevate Your Executive Presence: *Your Roadmap to Executive Excellence*
87. Smart Decisions: *Mastering Problem Solving with Strategic Solutions for Business Success*
88. Strategic Planning: *Developing and Implementing Strategic Plans to Achieve Long-Term Business Goals*
89. The Power of Stay Interviews
90. Developing G.R.I.T.
91. Adaptability
92. Diagnosis- *A Key Skill for Leadership*
93. The Burnout-Proof Salesperson: *The Master Guide to Preventing Stress & Burnout-* Strategies for Thriving in Sales
94. Learning from Failure: *Keys to Success*
95. Customer Success Management
96. Overcoming the Killers of Motivation
97. The C-Suite Code: *Mastering Skills for Executive Excellence'*

98. Dealing with Difficult Customers
99. Unlocking Your Potential: Mastering the Top 20 Life Skills for a Brighter Future
100. Nurturing Tomorrow's Leaders: *Essential Soft Skills Every Child Must Learn*
101. Lively & Fun Party Games for Seniors & Elders
102. Role Playing for Sales Champions: From Practice to Performance
103. Fun and Exciting Party Games for Kids
104. Case Studies for Sales
105. Role-Playing for Unbeatable Customer Service
106. Case Studies in Customer Service
107. Case Studies in Winning Negotiations
108. Case Studies in Management & Leadership
109. Case Studies in Human Resources & Talent Management
110. CEO Success Blueprint: The Essential Toolkit for CEOs and C-Level Executives
111. The Salesperson's Self-Coaching Guide: *Master Your Own Self-Coaching Plan for Success*
112. Overcoming Procrastination: *Your Ultimate Guide to Stop Delaying and Start Living Your Best Life*
113. When True Colors Are Exposed: *The Journey to Unmasking Humanity*
114. Life-Changing Habits for Teens: Teen Success Blueprint for a Bright Future
115. Workplace Stress-Free: *Proven Strategies to Thrive at Work and Beyond*
116. Objection Overruled: *The Ultimate Guide to Turning 'No' into 'Yes'"*
117. Building Strong Teams: *A Comprehensive Guide to Team Building*
118. Ethical & Moral Leadership in Business: Eliminating Unethical Practices & Building a Culture of Trust & Integrity
119. Rising Strong: Building Positive: High Self-Esteem for a Fulfilling Life-*A Practical Guide for Students, Employees, Leaders & Entrepreneurs*

From the Ministry side, Gerard graduated in the very first batch of Charis Bible College-India & had for over 9 years served as a Part-time Faculty at Charis Bible College-Chennai (Andrew Wommack Ministries-Colorado, USA).
He also holds a Diploma in Worship (a subject closest to his heart) from the JSOW and is also a graduate of the Advanced Mentorship Program (AMP) and the Circle Of Ministerial Engagement (C.O.M.E.) of Prophet Jerome Fernando and a Spiritual Son of the Esteemed Prophet.
An accomplished author of several Secular & Christian Books, Gerard has been on the board of a few international organizations and boasts of being the SON of the MOST HIGH GOD: An ordinary guy following an extraordinary GOD!

...And some of his most recent Christian Books being:

1. A Bouquet of Praises for My KING
2. Christian Jokes for the Serious Religious' Folks!
3. Jesus Healed You!
4. Praise24Ever! (also in Tamil version)
5. The 5G Network of GOD
6. Building Faith over F.E.A.R- FACE EVERYTHING AND RISE with JESUS
7. Hebrew and Greek Praise and Worship Words
8. Godly Mothers' and Grandmothers' Bible Story time for Kids!
9. Miracles of Jesus in Pictures
10. Raise your Praise all 365 Days
11. Thanking GOD with an Attitude of Gratitude
12. Meditating on the Attributes of GOD
13. Puppet Scripts
14. Alcohol Ruins, JESUS Reforms, Renews & Restores!
15. Habakkuk 2:2 Christian Daily Journal, Planner & Organizer
16. ABC of GOD's Word for Handwriting Practice
17. Daily Bible Verse Handwriting Practice (Building Godly Character & Faith through Cursive Handwriting Practice!)
18. Guiding Light: Fun & Faith-Building Bible Activities for Children
19. Rejecting Grasshopper Talk: From Grasshopper to Giant-Killer-*Defeating Giants Daily!*
20. Teen Titans of Faith: *Building Courage, Determination & Christ-like-Esteem*
21. I AM Empowered: *Unleashing Divine Power with Positive Declarations*
22. Be A Solution Provider-*From Passion to Purpose*: *A Biblical Guide to Being the Answer to the World!*
23. Miracles of JESUS
24. Parables of Jesus for a Meaningful Life!

25. A Grateful Heart: Importance of Sharing Testimonies of GOD's Grace
26. Melodies of Worship to JESUS: 31 Songs of Praise & Worship From My Heart to HIS!
27. I AM SO BLESSED!
28. My Daily Cup of Energizer
29. 31 Leadership Lessons *from* Jesus- *The Supreme Leader*
30. Peace Amidst Storms: A Biblical Guide to Conquering S.T.R.E.S.S.
31. Rise Above: 20 Biblical Eagle Lessons for Life's Triumphs
32. Godly Goal Setting: *The FAITHFUL Blueprint for a Purpose-Driven Life*
33. The Profound Attributes of our Mighty GOD: Understanding the 10S's of the Almighty
34. Worship Now, Worship Forever: *A Journey from Earthly Praise to Eternal Glory*
35. Unceasing Praise & Worship: *365 Days to Worship the King*
36. The ROAR Within: *Living with Purpose and Authority through the Power of the Holy Spirit*
37. From Potential to Purpose: Unlocking and Multiplying Your Talents & Gifts for Kingdom Impact
38. Songs from the Heart: *Worshipping GOD in Your Own Tune & Melody*
39. Awakening Praise & Worship: Hebrew & Greek Words to Raise Your Praise
40. Sing a NEW Song to the LORD Everyday: *Daily Devotions of Praise & Worship to Lift Your Heart & Glorify HIS Name*
41. *The* A.R.O.M.A. of True Worship: *Creating Worship That Delights God*
42. Becoming A Kingdom Champion: *Embracing God's Call for a Life of Purpose & Victory*
43. The Busy Businessman's Daily Devotional: 366 Crisp Truths to Start Your Day Strong
44. The Teacher's Heart: *Daily Devotions for Educators*
45. Anchored! *A 31-Day Devotional for Students Facing Life's Challenges*
46. Suddenly! Unlocking Unorthodox Breakthroughs through Unusual Worship
47. Overcoming Adversity: *Lessons from the Bible for Modern Challenges*
48. LORD, Don't do it without me
49. Kingdom Leadership: *Biblical Principles for Modern Leaders*
50. Heartprints of God- *Growing God's Way:* Daily Devotions for Kids to Shine Bright

51. Send Judah First: Let your Praises Go up First to See the Mighty Move of GOD
52. DIVINE MOMENTS: *Recognizing, Embracing, Preparing, and Walking into Life-Changing Encounters with God*
53. Be a Builder in the Kingdom: *The C.E.M.E.N.T. Guide to Creating a Lasting Legacy*
54. Unshakable: *Pillars of Godly Womanhood* (Pillars of Faith That Changed History)
55. Lead Like a Shepherd: *14 Essential Traits for Pastoral Excellence*
56. The Worship Leader's Arsenal: *Powerful Exhortations to Ignite Thanksgiving, Praise & Worship*
57. Women of UnShakable Faith: *31-Day Devotional for Strength, Purpose & Influence*
58. Called to Teach: *A Complete 10-Week Training Guide for Impactful VBS Teachers*
59. Strumming for the KING: Cowboy Songs of Faith & Fire
60. The Ultimate Youth Camp Playbook: *50 Bible-Centered Indoor Games to Engage, Equip, and Empower Teens*
61. Glad in HIS Presence: *David's Revelation of GOD's Love & Mercy*
62. The Spirit Behind the Sound: *52 Devotionals for Worship Teams*
63. THE COWBOY'S COMPASS: *Riding the Trail of Faith with Grit & Grace*
64. Worship as My Weapon: *Living Victoriously through the Power of Praise*
65. A Worshipper Always Wins*: Living a Life of Victorious Worship*
66. Worship That Leads to the Throne: *Practical Strategies for Worship Leaders to Inspire Their Team & Usher People into God's Presence*
67. Worship as Warfare: *Conquering through the Sound of Surrender*
68. Watchmen on the Walls: *A 31-Day Devotional for Worship Teams*
69. From Evening to Morning: *Rediscovering GOD's Sacred Hours*
70. KINGDOM BUSINESS: *52 Biblical Principles for GODLY Leadership & Wise Decisions*

Besides regularly contributing to business & trade journals, including international ones such as the 'Creative Training Techniques' and the 'Sales News' of the U.S.A, He is also a member of several prestigious bodies & trade associations, having participated in many Conferences & Workshops in India & Overseas.

Prior to his last assignment of leading & managing a large MNC as head, Gerard had a 3-year stint in the Middle East as a Consultant with a leading British Consultancy Firm.

As the past 'Official Country Representative' for the International Business Award- 'THE STEVIES'-(the business world's own Oscar) for about 4 years- he ensured a few Indian companies that qualify for the same every year!

Gerard can be contacted at:

Email: training@Sales-Training.in,training@CollectionSkills.com
Websites:

www.Sales-Training.in
www.EtiquetteWorks.in
www.CollectionSkills.com
www.RetailSalesTraining.in
www.SalesTrainingIndia.com
www.ManualPreparation.com
www.TrainingWithPuppets.com
www.FirstContactAcademy.com
www.SalesAndMarketingRecruiter.com

www.ingramcontent.com/pod-product-compliance
Ingram Content Group UK Ltd.
Pitfield, Milton Keynes, MK11 3LW, UK
UKHW021341190726
13845UKWH00027B/666

9 788198 926234